HOLMAN HUNT

THE LIGHT OF THE WORLD.
(*From the picture at Keble College, Oxford.*)

Bell's Miniature Series of Painters

HOLMAN HUNT

BY

GEORGE C. WILLIAMSON, Litt.D.

LONDON

GEORGE BELL & SONS

1902

A larger book on this artist is in preparation by the same author, which, however, will not be ready for some considerable time.

TABLE OF CONTENTS

LIST OF ILLUSTRATIONS

LIFE OF HOLMAN HUNT

WILLIAM HOLMAN HUNT was born in
April, 1827. His father was a ware-
houseman of London, who had passed his time
in the Manchester trade, and the boy was born in
Wood Street, Cheapside, in the heart of the City
of London.

His family were anxious that he should enter
one of the great manufacturing houses as a clerk
and follow in the steps of his father, but their
son was very unwilling to enter upon this kind of
life, and was eager to be an artist.

He had been removed from school when
between twelve and thirteen years of age, as he
had never shown much aptitude for study, and
employed most of his time in drawing in his copy-
books. The first place to which he was sent was
to an auctioneer and estate agent as a sort of
probationary clerk.

Fortunately for him, this employer was as much
interested in drawing as was the lad, and en-
couraged him in his pursuit ; but he was with him
only a year and a half, and then, at sixteen, he
became an assistant to the agents of Mr. R.
Cobden, a calico-printer of Manchester.

Here he found another clerk who was also fond

of drawing, and here it was that, having but little
to do, he amused himself, as he tells us, by so
cleverly drawing flies upon the ground - glass
window as to entirely deceive his employer, who
attempted one day, much to his discomfiture and
his pupil's amusement, to brush away the crowds
of painted flies which covered the window.

There was the greatest opposition at his home
to his becoming an artist, but he was allowed to
spend his small salary in taking lessons of a
portrait-painter in the City.

The desire, however, to take up the work pro-
fessionally became a passion with the lad, but its
accomplishment was a matter of grave difficulty.
The small savings of his father were at that time
broken into severely by a lawsuit, which reduced
them by half, and there was no money available
for a course of life which seemed to promise so
little emolument.

By painting portraits three days a week after
he left the Cobden office, he tells us he " managed
to pay expenses," and the remainder of his time
he gave to the British Museum Print-Room and
Sculpture-Gallery.

He tried to gain admission to the Academy
Schools, and was rejected twice. It was a hard
fight, and at length his father, giving him permission to try once more, told him definitely that
in case of failure he must come back to the City.

He tried for the third time, and was successful,
and in July, 1844, at the age of seventeen, got
into the schools as a probationer, and became a
student in January, 1845.

There he met Millais, who, although only fifteen, had already won the principal medal in the Antique School before he had gained admission to the Academy. Rossetti was at the same time a student in the schools. Holman Hunt's first picture sent to the Royal Academy, called *Hark!* (324), was not sold, nor was another which, about the same time, he sent in to the British Institution. The latter, called *Little Nell and her Grandfather*, now belongs to Mr. W. M. Rossetti; but the former, which he sold after the close of the show for a small sum, cannot now be found (see p. 61).

The next work which the young artist sent in was called *Dr. Rochecliffe performing Divine Service in the Cottage of Joceline Joliffe,* and was a scene from Scott's novel "Woodstock." This also cannot now be found. It was selected from the Royal Academy by the winner in an Art Union competition, for the value of £21, and passed to the winner, a Mr. Glendinning. Then came a still better picture, *The Flight of Madeline and Porphyro,* a scene from the "Eve of St. Agnes," by Keats. This also was sold by the Art Union, and won for £63 by a Mr. Bridger, but it cannot now be found. He also exhibited at Suffolk Street, in 1847, a picture called *Dead Mallard,* which cannot be traced. It would be most interesting to discover these four early works (see p. 62).

Then came the period of the Pre-Raphaelite Brotherhood, which is described in a succeeding chapter, and needs only to be mentioned here.

The next picture which marks a period is *The Hireling Shepherd*, which Holman Hunt painted after generous aid had been given him by his fellow-student Millais.

Up to this time the strain upon the mind of the young artist had been aggravated by the worry which his work was causing to his father. It had been suggested by some critics that the pictures exhibited were so bad that the Royal Academy would take steps, not only to remove them from their walls, but also to prevent the young band of artists from ever again competing ; and Mr. Hunt senior was often being laughed at for the work of his son, and told what a disgrace the lad was to his family. Holman Hunt himself was just then engaged, on the invitation of Dyce, in cleaning and restoring the wall-paintings that Dyce had done some years ago at the Trinity House, and so was earning money to pay his expenses ; but it seemed as though he would never be able to make any real position in art, and he was much disposed to drop the whole thing and emigrate to Canada.

Then came a generous offer of assistance from Millais, and the painting of *The Hireling Shepherd*, which was hung upon the line.

Valentine and Sylvia, which he painted a little later on, won a fifty-pound prize at Liverpool, and was then sold to a Belfast correspondent, who paid for it in monthly payments, and obliged the artist to take out some of the money which was due to him in the form of other paintings.

At about this time he was introduced to Mr.

and Mrs. Combe of Oxford, who continued to be his warm friends and patrons as long as they lived. They were afterwards the owners of *The Light of the World*, and bought many others of his works, which are now to be seen in the University Galleries at Oxford.

The Hireling Shepherd was sold through another friend, a Mr. Maude, to his cousin, Mr. Broderip, the magistrate and naturalist, for 300 guineas, 150 being paid at once, and the remainder in quarterly payments.

Mr. Broderip introduced him, so he tells us, to Sir R. Owen, and in that way started another friendship, which resulted in the fine portrait of the great palæontologist which Holman Hunt afterwards painted, and which he lent to the Glasgow Exhibition.

Then came the picture of *The Strayed Sheep* done for Mr. Charles Maude, a splendid example of an English landscape, and in the estimation of Mr. Ruskin—so he told a friend of the author's—the best painting of sheep that had ever been painted.

This was done near Hastings, and in this way acquired its earlier titles of *Our English Coasts*, or *Fairlight Downs*.

Edward Lear, the artist tells us, was his companion in his Fairlight lodgings when this work was done. Mr. Maude paid £120 for it, and the picture also gained for the artist a prize of £60 at the Birmingham Exhibition.

The same year saw the portrait of *Canon Jenkins* and the picture of *Claudio and Isabella*.

These successes enabled him to repay the advances made by Millais, and to clear off the greater part of the debt he owed to his landlady, and he tells us with that frankness which characterizes the whole of the biographical articles in the *Contemporary Review*—from which the chief of these facts are taken—that he "had suffered almost unbearable pain at passing her and her husband week after week, without being able to even talk of annulling his debts."

The Light of the World was the next picture exhibited, and this was purchased by Mr. Combe, who afterwards gave it to Keble College, Oxford, where it still hangs. He it was who took "the greatest interest in the project" that the artist had always planned, that he should journey to the East, and there paint some great Scriptural pictures.

Previous to this, however, he painted that remarkable picture called *The Awakening* (or *Awakened*) *Conscience*, which was commissioned by Mr. (afterwards Sir Thomas) Fairbairn, one of the very few commissions which the independent painter ever allowed himself to take, and accepted on this occasion only on the understanding that he was to have full liberty to treat the subject as he thought best.

This picture, which received the highest and perhaps somewhat extravagant praise from Ruskin, has always caused some sensation wherever it has been shown, and fully bears out the ideas of the painter as to the didactic value of a painting.

The Awakened Conscience, as the artist called

it at the Royal Academy Exhibition, was finished in January, 1854, and on the same night on which it was delivered Holman Hunt took train for Paris and set off on his long-promised journey to the East.

He was back in London in February, 1856, having been away two years and one month, and brought back with him " *The Scapegoat* quite complete," which had taken him eight months to paint, "about half a dozen water-colours finished, and another half a dozen nearly so."

Then came troubles and discouragement, as the picture of *The Scapegoat* would not sell, and eventually realized only a comparatively small sum. His father died about this time, and but for the encouragement given him by Mr. Combe and others, the result to the artist might have been serious.

His next great work was *The Finding of Christ in the Temple*, but that was, as he tells us, " often with its face to the wall while I was working at pot-boilers to get the means to advance it at all ;" eventually, however, by the generous and timely assistance of Mr. Combe, the work was completed, and sold to Mr. Gambart for a larger sum than had ever before been given for the work of an English artist—5,500 guineas.

A charming work painted at about this time was the one called *The Schoolgirl's Hymn*, which was shown at the French Gallery in 1859, but cannot now be found.

Back went Holman Hunt, after selling his great

picture, to the Holy Land, and the fruit of his
sojourn there has been seen ever since.

In 1861 he exhibited *The Lanternmaker's
Courtship*, one of the most brilliant little pictures
he has ever painted, and then, save for two
portraits, one of *A Child as Henry VIII.* and
the other of *The Right Honourable Stephen
Lushington*, there was nothing seen from his
brush during the five years from 1862 to 1866.

In 1867 he was still away, but he sent in to the
Academy his *Festival of St. Swithin*, now at
Oxford, and the *Il Dolce far niente*, a fine
striking portrait of a woman, brilliantly painted,
which now belongs to Mr. Thomas Brocklebank. He also completed his picture of *The
Marriage of the Princess of Wales*, which is now
at Oxford.

The same year also saw the completion of
Afterglow, which was painted in the East, and
Isabella and the Pot of Basil, in which he returned
to earlier ideas and tastes, resting for a time from
his Eastern pictures to take up anew the study
of Keats' poems.

A journey in Italy produced its fruit in *Salerno
Cathedral—Interior* and *Exterior*—of which the
Interior belongs to Mr. Craik ; in the *Camaldoli*,
which so delighted Ruskin and passed into his
possession, and now belongs to Mr. Severn ; and
in the *Maid of Tuscany*, which was so popular a
work when first exhibited.

To the Academy in 1869 Holman Hunt sent
in a picture called *The Birthday* and a portrait,
and then there was a pause again till 1874, while

the artist was busy at work upon *The Shadow of Death*.

This grand picture was completed in that year, but the only work sent to the Academy was the *Portrait of Mr. Fairbairn*, and from that time Holman Hunt has not exhibited within the walls of Burlington House.

His pictures have never been painted in a hurry. They have always been the result of immense toil and labour. He has put himself and his whole heart into them, worked for long periods, steadily building up his pictures in the most painstaking manner, and with every possible thought and attention to the smallest detail. For these reasons and because of his long absences from England it has been rumoured more than once that he was no longer living.

The Shadow of Death once completed, another great work was commenced ; but meantime he had joined the Old Water-Colour Society, though the society does not yet possess a diploma work from his hand. He first exhibited in that gallery in 1869, and sent in also a couple of paintings in 1870 and 1871. Then came a long break, and nothing was shown by him until 1879, although in 1877 he had shown four pictures at the newly-founded Grosvenor Gallery.

In 1879 we find at the Grosvenor Gallery that profoundly pathetic work *The Ship* and some water-colours at the Old Society. Then again for a while the Grosvenor Gallery had his work, and he showed portraits of his children and some studies in 1880, the *Portrait of Owen* in 1881, and a missing picture called *Miss Flamborough*, more in his earliest pre-Raphaelite manner, in 1882.

In 1883 there was a picture at the Old Water-Colour Society, and in 1884 his *Portrait of Rossetti* was shown at the Grosvenor Gallery, followed the next year by the lovely *Bride of Bethlehem*, which now belongs to Mr. Haslam, and then, with the exception of three small works at the Old Water-Colour Society, there is a break again, while the artist was at work at *Christ among the Doctors in the Temple*, about which he wrote an article in the *Contemporary Review*, and from which a mosaic was made for the chapel of Clifton College. This painting now belongs to Mr. Middlemore.

When the New Gallery was started, Holman Hunt, ever ready to try a new place, sent to it a *Portrait of Mr. Price*, following it the next year with the wonderful painting called *Sorrow*, one of the most profound works which he has ever painted, full of the most marvellous pathos.

The Water-Colour Society was, however, not forgotten, and *The Sleeping City* appeared there, as well as a revival of a very early idea called *Recollections of the Arabian Nights*, which he had already used many years before (1857) in the illustration he did for Moxon's edition of Tennyson.

He had not deserted the Grosvenor Gallery meantime, as in 1887 he exhibited there *Amaryllis* and the portrait of *Hilary as the Tracer*, both of which pictures are still in his own possession.

The Gallery had two shows of pastel work in

1888 and 1889, and to these Holman Hunt sent
portraits, those of his old friend, *R. B. Martineau*, a portrait which cannot be now traced,
and the one of *Mr. Combe* which is now at
Oxford.

He contributed to the winter exhibitions of
the Old Water-Colour Society at intervals since
1883, sending five pictures in that year, one only
in the following, four in 1886, one in 1889, one in
1890, and eleven in 1892, and then in 1893, after
exhibiting at the summer show *Sunset in the
Val d' Arno* and *Athens*, the fruit of more travels
in Europe, he retired from the Society altogether.

Since then it has been the New Gallery which
alone has presented his works to the public,
except on those occasions when he went to the
Fine Art Society to show single works, such as
the *Triumph of the Innocents*. His *Portrait of
Mr. Rathbone* was seen at the New Gallery in
1894; a portrait of another friend, *Mr. Sydney
Morse*, who owns *Asparagus Island* and other
works, was seen in 1898, together with the fine
picture called *The Beloved*, which is in the Royal
collection; and lately, in 1899, was presented the
last work which he has exhibited, namely, *The
Miracle of the Sacred Fire in the Church of the
Holy Sepulchre at Jerusalem*.

In connection with this work, it is worthy of
notice that although the artist has told us that
he did not think the subject had ever before been
treated, yet in the New Salon in Paris of the same
year was a picture of the identical event by

M. Girardet, taken from the gallery of the church, and called *Le Feu Sacré du Saint Sepulcre, Samedi Saint à Jerusalem.*

It is perhaps worth noting that the attention which Holman Hunt received was largely from the cultured merchants who resided in the North, and especially in the neighbourhood of Liverpool, that great port which can boast of a school of eminent artists all its own, and whose sons have always been famous for the patronage they have extended to the greater artists of England, but very notably to those who have formed the Pre-Raphaelite School.

Near Liverpool are to be found all the chief Pre-Raphaelite pictures, and the paintings done by the Liverpool landscape artists who followed the same teaching. It will be noticed that the chief of Holman Hunt's works are in Liverpool, Manchester, Birkenhead, Heswall, Birmingham, Harborne, Altrincham, and Allerton, and most of them are owned by merchants who have had business connections with the northern and western parts of England.

In black-and-white work Holman Hunt did a few very fine drawings for the edition of Tennyson issued by Moxon in 1857, and also some sound work for " Once a Week," " Good Words," " English Sacred Poetry," Watts' " Divine and Moral Songs," Gatty's " Parables from Nature," Dalziel's " Bible Gallery," and other books, and he prepared some delightful designs for " Pilgrim's Progress " and the " Holy War " which were never used as intended.

THE ART OF HOLMAN HUNT

MANY of the statements we wish to make as to the work of this artist will find a more fitting place in the chapter on our illustrations, when we come to consider seriatim the pictures illustrated in the book, but a few general words may here be desirable.

At the first glance most of the paintings by Mr. Holman Hunt are felt to be unpleasant in colouring and harsh in detail, and the effect which they produce, instead of being one of pleasure, is often the reverse.

This is occasioned by the determined desire of the artist to paint every colour as it appears actually to be, in the light in which he is regarding it, and in the limited vision that he takes of his subject at the moment.

The shadows, for example, in the fine landscape called *The Strayed Sheep* are painted in a somewhat raw blue, and there is no doubt, as has been pointed out by an eminent critic, that actually the colour is a correct one, and that if the shadow is so regarded through a pinhole in the blazing sunlight it will be found of exactly the hue that Hunt represents it. Herein, however, lies the error, which one of the ablest critics of

modern times—M. de la Sizeranne—has pointed
out.   In gazing at a landscape the eye does *not*
confine itself even at one moment to considering
the hue of one colour by itself, but it sees all
the landscape at the same time, and the effect
of one colour is modulated against another.
Absolute accuracy in the painting of a single
colour is apt therefore to lead the artist astray,
and it has done so in this case.   The colours are
accurate, and can be proved to be so ; the effect
of the light is true, and cannot be gainsaid ; but
the complete effect of the picture is lost in the
separate consideration given to individual parts,
and having been built up, as Mr. Quilter says,
" like a mosaic," it has much of the harshness
and hard outline of such work.

In technique the desire of the Pre-Raphaelite
men was to avoid the low tones and dark first
background which it was the custom of the
artists of their day to place upon their canvases.
Upon this were superimposed bright flecks of
colour, and in this way transparency was quickly
obtained with " delightful harmonies."

The Pre-Raphaelites began with a clean canvas
without any first preparation of background, and
laboriously built up the picture bit by bit, making
some of their effects by the juxtaposition of
colours, rather than by superposition, and finish-
ing each piece of the work ere " another was commenced, without retouching."

The consequence of this method of procedure,
notably in an artist who works so slowly as does
Holman Hunt, is the want of harmony which is

characteristic of his work, and the strange hard line and hard colouring which is so noticeable in it.

When the purpose which the artist has had in his mind all through—that of absolute truth—is understood, much of this may be forgiven; and to many persons the sight of a work by Holman Hunt has been the lesson they have needed in order to understand that there *are* in Nature the brilliant effects which he has painted, and which afterwards they are able to realize.

The ruddiness of many of the faces in the paintings, say, for example, in the *Hireling Shepherd*, arises from the same earnest desire for absolute truth, and the effect of the light is quite accurately depicted. The constant change of light, and the power which the air has of toning colours and modulating them, and which the eye possesses of combining colours into one harmonious whole, have, however, to be remembered, and it is then realized that although at a given second the colour may be and appear as it is painted, yet that the light and air and eye would conspire to prevent its being accepted in that hue, and all would be modulated down into a perfect harmony.

These lessons are far more difficult to remember when the painting is done entirely in the open air, as Holman Hunt does it. The eye then has to travel slowly over the roof or walls of the house which is being represented, measuring in its scrutiny each brick, or tile, or stone, while the hand is steadily recording, item by item, the details which the eye is examining. In this punctilious attention to minor details the general impression and effect of the whole in the atmosphere which surrounds it, is apt to be overlooked. If, however, preliminary colour sketches, studies of draperies, and careful drawings of detail, are made out of doors, and then the picture is painted in the studio, there is less chance of the broad atmospheric effect being missed.

Holman Hunt's work loses so much charm by reason of the labour which is so evident in it, the tightness of the brush work and its overscrupulous carefulness.

His finest colour schemes—and his colour at its best is superlatively fine—lose for the same reason, and there is a want of breadth that spoils the general effect.

His aim, however, is to be didactic, to be symbolic, and never to lose a single feature of his symbolism. He paints with precision—"dryly," as has been well said—but it is the very necessity of the case which obliges him to do so. His pictures are not for the ordinary purpose of giving pleasure. Some of them, in fact, have not that intention at all. They are not even painted in order to lift the spectator into another world of thought ; to create an emotion ; but rather to teach and to preach, and the poetry of the painter is crusted over with symbolism to such an extent that there is a danger of the poetry itself being lost.

Bright colours were demanded, elaborate symbolism, and absolute truth as to every separate feature ; stern, almost cruel reality, and the fettering of all other considerations in order that the main purpose of the picture should be clear and unerring.

To understand the art of Holman Hunt, all this must be kept well in mind, and then, and then only, will his greatest works be understood and his aim appreciated.

Hard work, devotion to duty, intense belief in religion, devoted attachment to the person and mission of Christ, and the consequent determination to use his art in order to teach others and to expound Scripture, are the main characteristics of this painter of Christian art, and the more ordinary methods of painting are all, by his intention, to be subordinated to these ruling forces of his character.

Permanence is, however, one of his aims, and no artist is more careful as to what colours he uses, and he has gone so far as to compound and grind many of them himself, in order that the paintings into which he has put the best of his skill during a long life, and intended as lessons to the world, should last as long as possible, and have no whit of their force removed by fading or alteration. True he knows and believes them to be ; they enshrine his dearest beliefs, and they contain his message to the world, and therefore, so far as he can see to it, they shall last in all their first brilliance to tell their story when he has long passed away.

THE PRE-RAPHAELITE BROTHER-HOOD

A FEW words are necessary in order to explain what were the aims and purposes of the remarkable group of artists to which Holman Hunt belonged.

In 1848, as Mr. W. M. Rossetti says, "the British School of Painting was in anything but a vital or lively condition."

It was represented by such men as Maclise, Landseer, Mulready, Leslie, Dyce, Cope, and Frith, but it "had sunk very far below what it had been in the days of Hogarth, Reynolds, Gainsborough, and Blake, and its ordinary average had come to be something for which commonplace is a laudatory term, and imbecility a not excessive one."

It had left the study of Nature and exact representation. It had few ideas either in art or in character, and its works were mostly sentimental, formal and prim ; absurdly classical, or else distinguished by baldness of design and lack of imagination.

It was especially the absence of the ring of honest truth about the pictures of the day in their cloysome richness, and in their prettiness and melodrama, which offended the better taste of certain youthful artists of the time, of whom Holman Hunt was one.

Their eyes were not closed to the existence of some good work which was being done. They recognised the sweet simplicity of Leslie, the sense of country life which existed in Collins, the magnificent colour-sense which was the special charm of the work of Etty, the clear, good draughtsmanship of Maclise, and the painstaking work of Mulready ; but they could not find in any of them that honest independence, coupled with intention to enunciate with truth and accuracy, the message which should dwell in the soul of every true artist.

There was even in the taste of the day as regards the Old Masters the same fault to be found, and the paintings of Guido, Parmigiano, Sasso Ferrato, Carlo Dolce, and Domenichino, were those in greatest repute, while the earlier, truer, and more independent masters were under a cloud.

It was then that three young men—Holman Hunt, who was but twenty-one years of age ; John Everett Millais, who was nineteen ; and Dante Gabriel Rossetti, who was twenty—all of them students, full of enthusiasm, decided to make a strong and bold effort to break through the chains of convention which bound them, and go back to Nature for inspiration, and paint truly and honestly what they saw and what they believed was right.

These three it was who created the P.R.B., and were its first members. To them was added later Thomas Woolner, a sculptor of twenty-two years of age, the eldest of the group, and then later on three other men — James Collinson, a domestic painter, who died in 1881 ; Frederic George Stephens, an Academy student of painting ; and William Michael Rossetti, a Government clerk, brother of D. G. Rossetti.

The last two devoted their attention to literature, and did not paint. They are still living, but Woolner died in 1892, Millais in 1896, and Rossetti in 1882, so that of the original seven, three only remain.

The little organization which was formed by these seven men was one of protest and reform ; "they meant revolt," as has been well said, "and they produced revolution." No movement in art has ever had such far-reaching results. Beginning with a few young men, it influenced the whole art of the country, and extended to Europe, and it is very much to its bold determination that we owe the importance of the British School of Art in the present day.

Many men were intimate with the P.R.B. members, and associated with them in their work, notably Ford Madox Brown, who was far older than any of them, but who did not join their association, and was, as has been said, "more influenced by them than influencing them."

It is, however, at the same time impossible to overlook the very important part that Madox Brown had in inspiring the very work which was characteristic of the P.R.B. Mr. Quilter says that he was "in all but name the real founder and leader of the movement." Mr. Stephens states that there can be "no doubt that to Brown's guidance and example we owe the better part of Rossetti as a painter *per se*," and Bell Scott adds that "Rossetti with much effusion acknowledged his indebtedness to Brown for many lessons that he had given him."

It is therefore certain, as M. de la Sizeranne has most clearly laid down, that although Brown, who disliked cliques and was "sceptical as to the utility of coteries," did not associate himself with the younger men, he was not only the teacher of Rossetti, but was to a large extent responsible for the very opinions incorporated in the action taken by the P.R.B. Much of the enthusiasm which attended their opening efforts was due to him, and the persistent instruction that it was to Nature they were to go for guidance, was certainly his.

The names of such men as Arthur Hughes, C. A. Collins, Deverell, Bell Scott, Hancock, J. R. Herbert, and Patmore, will also be recalled as associated with the P.R.B.; but none of them were actual members, and the three great painters in the Brotherhood were Holman Hunt, Millais, and Rossetti, and it is their influence which has produced this marked result.

They called themselves by the name of the Pre-Raphaelite Brotherhood, as they entertained a "deep respect and sincere affection for the works of the artists who had preceded Raphael, and they thought that they should more or less be following the lead of these artists if they themselves were to develop their own individuality, disregarding school rules."

That they were altogether wise in their actions cannot be maintained. Many of their ideas were crude and ill-formed, some of their sympathies were unwise, some of their prejudices inconsiderate ; but in their independent study of Nature they had a firm basis of what is right in art, and their honest truth gained the day, while the excrescences due to youthful ambition and unwise enthusiasm disappeared in due time.

The three artists were very different men. Holman Hunt, as he himself has said, "was a steady, and even enthusiastic worker, trained by a long course of early difficulties, and determined to find the right path for his art."

Rossetti, "with his spirit alike subtle and fiery, was essentially a proselytizer . . . possessed of an appreciation of beauty of the most intense quality."

Millais, says Mr. Hunt, stood "in some respects midway between us, showing a rare combination of extraordinary artistic faculty with an amount of sterling English common-sense," and he was, it must be mentioned, the only one of the group who at that time had anything in the way of means behind him.

The three artists worked together, and it is their work alone which need concern us, for Woolner went to Australia, and never did any painting at all, confining his attention to sculpture ; Collinson resigned his membership, and the others, as already stated, devoted their energies to literature rather than to art.

The actual brotherhood lasted for a very short time, perhaps three years or so, as it was not considered desirable to flaunt in the face of the public, initials received with so much derision at first, and considered as the emblems of revolution. Very few pictures bore the mystic initials, but such as they were their merit was remarkable.

The first were those that appeared in the exhibitions of 1849: *Lorenzo and Isabella*, by Millais, *Rienzi*, by Holman Hunt—both hung just above the line at the Royal Academy—and the *Girlhood of Mary Virgin*, by Rossetti, which either from choice or necessity was hung at the so-called Free Exhibition held in a gallery at Hyde Park Corner.

These were the starting-points of the movement, and they were received favourably on the whole, the *Times* giving a lengthy comment to them, and noting them as the remarkable feature of the exhibitions.

Millais's picture, which Mr. Holman Hunt declares "the most wonderful painting that any youth still under twenty ever did in the world," was sold before his show-day; Rossetti's picture was also sold; but *Rienzi* was not bought for some time, until a Mr. Gibbons—who really never valued the work, but hid it away in a cupboard —purchased it for £100.

The outburst of feeling, however, which was to reward the P.R.B. for their efforts, had already commenced in artistic circles, and broke out in full volume in the following year.

In 1850 Hunt exhibited his *Converted British Family*, Millais his *Christ in the House of His Parents*, and Rossetti his *Ecce Ancilla Domini* (in the same gallery as before, although it had that year been removed into Portland Place), and all the pictures were vehemently attacked and condemned.

Still, however, the complete force of the attack was not realized, but how bitter it could be was seen when an article against the picture by Millais appeared from Charles Dickens in *Household Words*.

Millais had by then sold his picture, but Holman Hunt had not been so fortunate, and it was not disposed of until after the close of the exhibition.

Another year came round, and Millais sent to the Royal Academy, *Mariana in the Moated Grange*, the *Return of the Dove to the Ark*, and the *Woodman's Daughter ;* Holman Hunt sent *Valentine rescuing Sylvia from Proteus*, and Collins a *portrait* of a Mr. Bennett and a picture called *Convent Thoughts ;* while two scenes from *Beatrice at the Marriage Feast* constituted the work of Rossetti.

Then appeared the scornful article in the *Times* in May, 1851, which roused the indignation of Ruskin, and his celebrated letter of May 13 speedily showed that the effort which had been made by the three courageous young men had found one valuable supporter, and that his powerful interest had been enlisted on their side.

Ruskin refers to the labour bestowed upon the

VALENTINE RESCUING SYLVIA FROM PROTEUS.

(*From " The Two Gentlemen of Verona."*)

works, to their fidelity to truth, to their accuracy in matters of perspective, and to the earnestness and completeness of their studies of draperies.

His words are very forcible, and worth quoting in this place. "There is not," he said, "one single error in perspective in four, out of the five pictures in question, and in Millais's *Mariana* there is but one ; and I will undertake, if need be, to point out and prove, a dozen worse errors in perspective in any twelve pictures containing architecture taken at random, from among the various works of the popular painters of the day."

Further on he stated that "there is not a single study in the whole Academy, be it in works large or small, which for perfect truth, power, and finish could be compared for an instant with the black sleeve of the *Julia* or with the velvet on the breast and the chain-mail of the *Valentine* of Mr. Hunt's picture, or with the white draperies on the table of Mr. Millais's *Mariana*, and of the right-hand figure in the same painter's *Dove returning to the Ark*."

Finally he stated that "both as studies of drapery and of every minor detail, there has been nothing in art so earnest or so complete as these pictures since the days of Albert Dürer."

Ruskin followed up this letter with another, dated May 30, in which he wishes them "all heartily good-speed, believing in sincerity that if they temper the courage which they have shown in the adoption of their systems, with patience and discretion in framing it, and if they do not suffer themselves to be driven by harsh or careless criticism, into rejection of the ordinary means of obtaining influence over the minds of others; they may as they gain experience lay in our England the foundations of a school of art, nobler than the world has seen for three hundred years."

In these noble and prophetic words Ruskin accepted the challenge which the *Times*, with its remarks about "affected simplicity, senile imitation of a cramped style, false perspective, crude colours, morbid infatuation, and the sacrifice of beauty, truth, and genuine feeling, to mere eccentricity," had thrown down, and right gloriously defeated the challenger with his own words.

It was, as Holman Hunt says, "as thunder out of a clear sky," and it turned the current of public opinion. Up to that time all the papers, with the exception of the *Spectator*, which had accepted the defence of the cause written by W. M. Rossetti, and *Punch*, which had always, in the most remarkable manner, supported the artist, even though no pictures at the time so easily lent themselves to caricature, had been against the Brotherhood; but now it was seen that there was something to be said for the effort, curious as it appeared to be.

The revolt had been made, and there was no need any longer for pictures to be signed with the mystic initials P.R.B., but it must not be thought that all the world was won over at a bound.

Holman Hunt himself was dispirited at the failure of his picture, and had so much difficulty in selling his paintings, and in raising the necessary means for life and work, that he seriously proposed to drop painting altogether and emigrate to Canada as a farmer. He felt that, now the words of Ruskin had been said, he was no longer a disgraced man, as he had been called in the earlier part of the struggle, and that therefore, having found out that the "world he wanted to influence was not ready to be led," he could with an honest intention take up some other source of occupation.

Thanks, however, to the encouragement given to him by Millais, and thanks especially to the generous way in which the more successful artist assisted the less fortunate one, these gloomy ideas were dismissed, and Holman Hunt, with the cordial aid and sympathy of the father and mother of Millais, went down into Surrey with his friend, and both of them started on new works, Millais to do his remarkable *Ophelia*, and Holman Hunt his no less striking *Hireling Shepherd*.

A little later on the art critic on the *Times* was removed, and Tom Taylor took his place, and from that time the sympathy of the public was much more with the Pre-Raphaelites, and the victory could be counted as won.

The little organization had come to an end. Each artist was developing along his own lines and in his own way, and was showing what there was in him, but the need for concerted action had been demonstrated, and the claim which had been put in for truth, independence, and honest work had been accepted.

It will not be right to close this chapter without

a few words on the organ of the movement, which, like the society itself, lasted so short a time, but which in its brief career had so great an influence, not only upon art, but also upon literature.

The *Germ*, as it was at first styled, was suggested by Rossetti in 1849, near to the time of the closing of the exhibitions. "He alone," says Mr. W. M. Rossetti, "had already cultivated the art of writing in verse and in prose to some noticeable extent, and he was better acquainted than any other member with British and foreign literature." The other members were "all reading men, but not any of them had as yet done anything worth mentioning in writing."

It was from a book in the house of Millais, containing engravings of the frescoes in the Campo Santo at Pisa, which each had examined, that the very idea of the Brotherhood arose, but now it was also suggested that the society should have its own mouthpiece.

It was to be a monthly venture, priced at a shilling a number; each issue was to contain one etching, if not two; all the P.R.B.'s were to "be joint proprietors of the magazine," and W. M. Rossetti was appointed as the editor.

The original title invented by Rossetti was *Thoughts towards Nature*, a phrase which, as Mr. W. M. Rossetti wisely says, "although somewhat extra peculiar, indicated accurately enough the predominant conception of the P.R.B., that an artist, whether painter or writer, ought to be bent upon defining and expressing his own personal thoughts, and that these ought to be based upon a direct study of Nature and harmonized with her manifestations."

On December 19, 1849, however, there was a meeting of all concerned at Rossetti's studio, at which several other persons who were personal friends of the famous seven were present, and it was then decided that the chief title of the new magazine should be the *Germ*, and that the original title should be still used as a subordinate description.

The first issue came out early in January, 1850, but it did not sell well. No. 2, with a smaller edition, was issued in the following month, but its success was even slighter than that of its predecessor, and the resources of the little band were at an end.

The printers, however, came to the rescue, and the title was altered to *Art and Poetry; being Thoughts towards Nature, conducted principally by Artists;* and another firm of publishers agreed to have their name joined to that of the first firm who issued the paper.

In these altered circumstances two more parts were issued, No. 3 in March and No. 4 in May, and then the magazine died. The four parts form a most interesting series, and contain many things of really permanent value. Each part had an etching, the four being executed by Holman Hunt, James Collinson, Ford Madox Brown, and W. H. Deverell respectively, and the numbers contained, amongst other interesting literature, the story "Hand and Soul" and the poem "The Blessed Damozel," by Rossetti; "The Seasons," by Patmore ; " Dreamland," and other works, by Christina Rossetti ; and works by Madox Brown, Bell Scott, Collinson, F. G. Stephens, Alex., Geo. and John Tupper, Woolner, Orchard, and the editor.

The drawing by Holman Hunt is a very sweet one. It is in two divisions. In the upper part of it there are two lovers together in a meadow by a pool of water ; she is kneeling, in order to reach some flowers, and he is tenderly shielding her from harm. In the lower portion of the picture he alone is to be seen, extended at full length on the ground, with his face pressed deeply into the fresh mould of a grave ; behind him, in the distance, the nuns are passing, singing " Dies iræ " and " Beati mortui," and the bell is sounding close to him as he lies quiet on the earth. There is a volume of meaning in the drawing ; it is a poem expressed with the pencil.

The whole set of four issues has lately been reproduced in facsimile, with an important history of the magazine by its original editor, from which most of the facts just mentioned are taken.

OUR ILLUSTRATIONS

THE eight illustrations selected for this volume will depict the progress of the art of Mr. Holman Hunt from his early days down to recent times, and will illustrate not only the bold work of his youthful Pre-Raphaelite painting, but also the determination with which through all his long career he has followed the lines which he had laid for himself at its beginning.

They will also serve to show on what a strong basis of religious belief he has worked, and that his most notable pictures are those which have religious scenes depicted in them, and which possess that didactic quality that he has so steadily aimed to produce.

Valentine rescuing Sylvia was the picture exhibited in the Royal Academy in 1851 which so roused the temper of the critic for the *Times*, and produced the famous epistle from Ruskin to which allusion has already been made (see p. 24).

The scene is represented in the full blaze of sunlight, with the colours clear and distinct as they would have appeared in the circumstances.

Valentine stands in the centre, having come upon the scene just at the opportune moment

when Proteus, the treacherous lover who had tried
to supplant him in the affections of Sylvia, and
who had been the means of the persecution and
flight of the girl, had taken the advantage of her
defenceless condition to urge his suit.

Valentine has rescued her from the demands of
Proteus, and has called upon the craven lover to
apologize, and he, kneeling upon the ground, has
expressed his sorrow in such full and earnest
manner that Valentine, deeming his contrition
genuine and his love for Sylvia a very real affection, has relinquished in the most generous terms
his attachment to Sylvia, and has uttered the fateful
words: "All that was mine in Sylvia I give to thee!"

Julia, however, who stands by, still dressed in
the page's costume in which she had followed her
false lover, is overcome by the state of affairs, and
seeing that all her efforts will be in vain, and that
the man whom she loved would basely transfer
his affections to Sylvia, is on the point of fainting
away, and, nervously playing with her ring, leans
against the stem of a tree, striving to control her
feelings and not give way to the emotion that fills
her breast.

It has been suggested that Rossetti stood for
the head of Valentine; but that is not the case, as
Mr. Holman Hunt himself states that one " James
Hannay (now [1886] a magistrate in Australia)
sat for the head of Valentine, and a young
barrister, already well known amongst journalists,
and since greatly distinguished as a Cabinet
Minister in the Antipodes, was good enough to
let me paint Proteus from his posing."

The colour scheme of the picture is remarkable, its brilliance splendid, and the technique cannot be surpassed, as it is built up bit by bit with a firm, dexterous hand, and is still in perfect order.

Ruskin expressed regret that the faces of Sylvia and Julia were not more lovely, and that Proteus had not a finer head; but the character of the man is very well typified by his features, and the grand dignity of Valentine and the timid, nervous struggle of emotion discernible in the features of Julia redeem the picture from this adverse criticism.

The pose of Valentine is a striking one, and the whole conception is instinct with life and movement, but it is in its quality of absolute truth that its greatest merit consists.

The blaze of light, the accuracy of the shadows, the stern reality of the effect of strong sunlight and glowing heat, and the independence of the grouping and conception of the scene, all contribute to the impressiveness of the picture.

It was painted at Sevenoaks, in the woods of Knole, the armour was lent to the young artist by Mr. Frith, and the lady who sat for the figure of Sylvia was Miss Siddall, who afterwards became the wife of Dante Gabriel Rossetti. The Julia was painted from a model.

Every detail is painted with the most unswerving truth, and the picture is a notable example of the attitude which the young band of workers had taken up, of going direct to Nature and depicting everything as it actually would appear. The painting is luminous in tone, searching in finish, and full of vigour.

The Hireling Shepherd, which followed this one in the succeeding year, was the first which Holman Hunt had upon the line at the Royal Academy.

It is an allegory, somewhat laboured and confused, and slightly melodramatic and artificial; but it is a fine piece of painting, and full of symbolism used in the striking way which Holman Hunt favours.

The hireling shepherd has neglected his flock, and is idling with the rough, careless girl who lolls upon the grass near to him. The sheep, left to their own devices, are wandering off into a neighbouring cornfield, and eating the green corn, which is poison to them.

In his hand the man is holding a death's-head moth, from which the woman shrinks with superstitious dread, while so absolutely indifferent is she to duty that the very lamb which she has taken on her lap is allowed to regale itself upon unripe green apples without rebuke.

The man and woman are just simply rustics —strong, rough, and coarse in expression; the scene of the picture is the meadow in full sunlight. Nothing is tempered, nothing is obscured; all is seen in the intense white light of the afternoon.

Never was harder, sterner truth seen in any painting, and, like *Summer Heat* of Madox Brown, the picture almost makes the spectator blink with the brightness of the light.

By permission of the Corporation of Manchester.]

THE HIRELING SHEPHERD.

The almost cruel truth of the picture, from a painter's point of view prevents it from being a pleasant or satisfying work.

The intense blue of the shadows, although absolutely accurate, is repellent, and although the trees are painted in masterly manner, as trees are very seldom painted, and as certainly they were not painted in the fifties, yet the effect of the crude greens in them, the exaggerated redness of the faces, and the radiant effulgence of the light, all need to be understood before the high merit of the work can be appreciated.

The picture was frankly allegorical, and was painted, said the artist, " in rebuke of the sectarian vanities and vital negligences of the day"; and by this frank avowal much criticism was raised as to whether an artist had any right to take up so didactic a position, and to illustrate in this way the actions of certain careless shepherds, and so cast blame upon all.

As an allegory the picture has its clear, defined meaning; as a painting it is unusually true, faithful, and independent; but as a picture to hang in a gallery or a room it is not felicitous, nor is it charming.

It has to be judged by its own canons, and by the intention that the artist had in view when he painted it.

We now come to what has been undoubtedly the most popular picture which the artist has ever wrought. Not that Holman Hunt has ever striven after popularity, but it would have been strange

if he had not rejoiced when it came to him un-
bidden.

The Light of the World is, like the last work
mentioned, an allegory.

Here the lines are clearer and more ready of
definition. Ruskin called it " the most perfect
instance of expressional purpose that the world
has yet produced." In his letter to the *Times*
he explained the meaning of the picture in these
words :

" On the left of the picture is seen the door of
the human soul. It is fast barred; its bars and
nails are rusty; it is knitted and bound to its
stanchions by creeping tendrils of ivy, showing
that it has never been opened. A bat hovers
over it ; its threshold is overgrown with brambles,
nettles, and fruitless corn. . . . Christ approaches
it in the night-time. . . . He wears the white robe,
representing the power of the Spirit upon Him ;
the jewelled robe and breastplate, representing
the sacerdotal investiture ; the rayed crown of
gold, interwoven with the crown of thorns ; not
dead thorns, but now bearing soft leaves, for the
healing of the nations. . . . The lantern carried
in Christ's left hand is the light of conscience....
Its fire is red and fierce ; it falls only on the
closed door, on the weeds that encumber it, and
on an apple shaken from one of the trees of the
orchard, thus marking that the entire awakening
of the conscience is not merely to committed, but
to hereditary, guilt. This light is suspended by a
chain, wrapt about the wrist of the figure, showing that the light which reveals sin to the sinner

appears also to chain the hand of Christ. The light which proceeds from the head of the figure, on the contrary, is that of the hope of salvation; it springs from the crown of thorns, and, though itself sad, subdued, and full of softness, is yet so powerful that it entirely melts into the glow of it the forms of the leaves and boughs which it crosses, showing that every earthly object must be hidden by this light, where its sphere extends."

As the artist himself had never given his own explanation of the picture, and was at the time of its exhibition absent in the East, this glowing rendering of the inner meaning of the allegory was welcomed by the more thoughtful spectator, and served to bring at once into notice the remarkable work, with its solemn, pathetic, and majestic central figure.

The allegorical treatment of the subject lent itself to yet fuller explanation of details.

Other admiring critics pointed out that the sevenfold character of the lantern, every opening of which had its own special and different shape, was symbolical of the diversities of gifts the result of the same Spirit; that the fallen apple was a symbol of the fallen condition of man; that the hemlock in its dead state, as it has towered up at the door, was an emblem of brief pleasure with a bitter end, or of torpor and of poison, and so on; but the great central thought that the picture was intended to teach derived very little added force from these more or less fanciful interpretations.

The picture was a sermon, and was intended to be one. It was impressive and symbolical, and it has no doubt assisted many persons to a fuller appreciation of the great lesson which the artist desired to teach.

It was painted with all the indomitable courage that has ever characterized Mr. Hunt, working as he did by the rays of moonlight at the window of his London lodging, night after night, for many weeks, and from a painter's point of view it is a remarkable performance.

Perhaps it has looked better in reproductions in black and white than it ever did in its original colour, for, with all his love of full colour, Holman Hunt has never been gifted with a power of blending so as to soothe and compose the spectator.

On the contrary, he frequently rouses antagonism by his work, and when to this is added the laborious built-up appearance which many of his pictures have, owing to their minuteness of detail and the visible effort with which they have been executed, we have a result which in colour often militates against the pleasantness of the work.

There is no toil spared upon the picture, either in the thinking out or in the execution ; it is serious, it is impressive, it gives us a part of the artist's own life and thought; but through this very seriousness and labour there comes an effect of strain and heaviness, and a want of sympathy, which can never be overlooked.

It will be found, as we pursue our way through all the eight selected works, that this fault, if it

THE SCAPEGOAT.

be a fault, exists in every one of them, and that the artist, who has put himself into his works with such strong enthusiasm and determined feeling, has not always done so with discretion, and by his very labour has injured the effect which he desired to produce.

In his lighting he is always unusual. In the picture before us we have light from the unseen moon ; light from the stars ; light from the head of the Saviour ; light from the lantern ; and a strange luminous quality from the grains of frost on the ground, together with rays of reflection from the gems in the robe.

All these are less wearisome to the eye in the reproduction of the picture than in the original, and the work gains in harmony thereby, and no doubt from this reason became one of the most popular religious pictures which was ever painted.

In *The Scapegoat* the symbolism is not so laboured, and is confined to the effect of the creature that gives its name to the picture, rather than to any details connected with it.

In this way the picture has gained immeasurably in force over *The Light of the World*. We have also, in considering it, to give our attention to a marked characteristic of the artist, which has tinged all his succeeding works—namely, his belief that Scriptural scenes can only be adequately presented if the work of painting them is done in the Holy Land itself.

The intense belief in the doctrines of Christianity which is held by Mr. Holman Hunt must never be overlooked in considering his character or his actions. It is the mainspring of his life, and, as he himself states, " I wish always to paint, as men are supposed to write, what I believe."

The subject of *The Scapegoat* had, he said, much struck him when he had been searching Leviticus for the ceremonies of Jewish worship, with the idea of preparing for quite another picture, and he went out to Egypt in 1854 with the intention of producing some important works which he had planned.

It was the " time of the Crimean War, all the troops had been withdrawn from Syria, and the whole country was in disorder." It must also be remembered that European visitors to the East were then much more scarce than they are now ; there were none of the pleasant arrangements which now exist, and which make travelling in the Holy Land as comfortable as journeying in any part of Europe.

In the early part of the year the artist was in Cairo, the Pyramids, and Jerusalem, making many sketches, and "swimming," as he expresses it, " in the extraordinary new life in which he was."

He found the background which he wanted for his picture when on a trip to the Dead Sea with a friend, a Mr. Beaumont, of Warrington, and in October he set out alone, with Arabs to guard him and his tent, to Oosdom, on the "margin of the sea of Lot," and there set to work.

His experiences, which he narrates, with many

an interesting episode, in an article in the *Contemporary Review*, were exciting and troublous, and he had many narrow escapes before he got back to Jerusalem with his picture.

He only sketched in the goat, which died in the desert, giving all his attention to the wild and desolate landscape around; but in Jerusalem he completed the goat, and so finished the picture, besides working earnestly at the picture of *Christ in the Temple*, to which we shall refer later on.

Back he came in February, 1856, having exhausted nearly all his small stock of money, but he met with a chilling reception; and although *The Scapegoat* was hung on the line in the Academy; was mentioned by Lord Palmerston in his speech at the dinner; had the advantage of a special leader in the *Times*, and was talked about all over the country, it did not sell, and it was a long time before he was able to find a purchaser for a work which has lately become one of the best-appreciated of the artist's paintings.

None of his works suffer more in reproduction into black and white than does this one, and it is in this respect a contrast to those that have just been mentioned.

One of its greatest charms consists in the magnificence of its colouring, in which, what has been well called "the glow and witchery and opalescence of the Eastern lights towards the sunset" are so well depicted.

Ruskin speaks of "the salt sand of the wilderness of Ziph where the weary goat is dying. The neighbourhood," he adds, "is stagnant and pestiferous, polluted by the decaying vegetables brought down by the Jordan in its floods, and the bones of the beasts of burden that have died by the way of the sea, lie like wrecks upon its edge, bared by the vultures and bleached by the salt ooze."

Here it was that the artist pitched his tent and worked for many months in imminent peril of his life, painting the "purple crags of Moab and the pale ashes of Gomorrah."

The scene was a most suitable one in which to represent the wandering sin-stricken goat, dedicated to Azazel, the demon of the wilderness, and bearing upon its head the sins of the nation, carried away "out of sight of Jehovah as a vicarious sufferer for the sins" of the people.

The region was desolate, dreary, and unhealthy, "white with saline efflorescence," and was scarcely ever visited, being shunned even by the superstitious Arabs, who regarded it as haunted with evil spirits.

The poor, miserable, dying goat arouses in the minds of all who gaze at the picture the thought of the vicarious sacrifice of the Christ, of whom the goat, which "shall bear upon him all their iniquities into a land not inhabited," was the emblem.

As a piece of painting it is one of Hunt's least important works; as an allegory it ranks very high indeed.

Ruskin was one of the first to point out that it had too much feeling, too devoted an enthusiasm, and too little handling, and the criticism was a

THE FINDING OF THE SAVIOUR IN THE TEMPLE.

fair one. Its manipulation is not up to the usual
ability of the artist, the grouping is not successful,
and the actual technique is not up to the average,
but as a courageous piece of work done in great
peril, with a single aim and with a stern purpose,
it has the greatest importance.

It may be mentioned that there are two exist-
ing examples of this picture—one, the larger, which
now belongs to Sir Cuthbert Quilter, and a small
replica, which was until lately in the possession
of Lord Brassey, but cannot now be traced.

The Finding of Christ in the Temple was the
main work upon which Holman Hunt was engaged during this same period, but there were
innumerable difficulties in the way of its completion.

It was almost impossible at one time to get
the Jewish men, whom he desired to introduce
as the Rabbis, to sit to him, and he had all the
way through his progress to keep secret from
them the actual subject of the painting. It was
the "first Semitic presentment of the Semitic
Scriptures," but the trouble with the Semitic
sitters at one time threatened to prevent the
execution of the picture.

It was reported that the painter had come " to
traffic with the souls of the faithful." He was
forbidden to have any Jews in his studio, and
only half the work was completed in the City of
Zion, and the picture brought back incomplete to
London.

There, by the help of models, whom he ob-

tained in the Jewish schools, the picture was
finished, the figures of the Blessed Virgin and
Christ being left till the last, and then done
"from a lady of the ancient race, distinguished
alike for her amiability and beauty, and a lad in
one of the Jewish schools, to which the husband
of the lady furnished a friendly introduction."

The distinguishing executive character of the
picture which strikes the eye at first is its luminous
depth and intensity of colour, "the perfect truth
of the chiaroscuro that gives relief and roundness
to every part."

In more detailed examination, one is struck by
the delight and tenderness of that countenance
which reveals the yearning anxiety, the result of
three long days of searching with ever-increasing
fear.

Then the wistful, thoughtful, radiant look of
the Christ and His heedfulness of His mission,
which prevent His giving full attention to the
embrace of His mother, should be realized, and
the diversified countenances of the Rabbis studied,
one by one.

The picture is crowded with thought. The
scene is presented as a true one, in actual
Oriental garb, with all the accessories that doubtless surrounded it in actual life, and the trembling,
anxious mother, finding her devoted Son in the
midst of those venerable men, whom He had
been astonishing by His learning and His ques-
tions, is vividly depicted before our eyes.

In technique this is one of the artist's best
pictures.

ISABELLA AND THE POT OF BASIL.

It is not overdone with detail, albeit every attention is given to the accuracy of each accessory. Its colour is full and glorious, golden with sunlight and glowing with gemlike radiance, and all the grand colours and the gold and marble that appear in it are united in dexterous manner into one harmonious whole.

Symbolism is not lacking in the painting. There are money-changers, lads with lambs for sale, others driving out the intruding doves, women, and beggars, all having their part to take in the scene of the picture and in the lesson that it has to convey, but they are not so apparent as in other works, and the main fact of the painting is therefore not obscured in any way.

It is as well that one of our illustrations should be taken from the few really romantic subjects that Holman Hunt has ever attempted to illustrate, and that for once we should get away from the Scriptural scenes which embrace all his chief works.

In *Isabella and the Pot of Basil*, a picture which he did not send to the Royal Academy, or to any of the chief Galleries, but exhibited independently, we have a theme which may well have aroused all his ambition.

He had always been familiar with the poems of Keats, and had loved them, and from the very first the idea of the Pre-Raphaelite Brotherhood was to illustrate scenes from the poems which appealed to them so much, and which were in their time so little known or studied.

In this picture we have the story of "Fair Isabel, poor, simple Isabel," who passionately loved Lorenzo, "a young palmer in Love's eye."

She was the sister of two wealthy Venetian merchants, who had other aims with regard to their sister. He was their trusted clerk.

The brothers became acquainted with the passion that their sister had for Lorenzo, and with the way in which they shared the "fragrance of each other's heart," and they resolved to "cut Mercy with a sharp knife to the bone," and to kill Lorenzo in some dim forest and there bury him. To Isabel they told some story of his detention in the far country to which they had sent him, and she waited for his return, wondering "what dungeon climes could keep him off so long."

At length one night he stood before her "in the drowsy gloom," and from his "lorn voice, as in a palsied Druid's harp unstrung," she learned the tale. Into the forest secretly she went, and there, where "red whortleberries droop above my head, and a large flint stone weighs upon my feet," she found his body and brought away with her his head.

This ghastly treasure she wrapped in a "silken scarf, sweet with the dews of precious flowers plucked in Araby," and buried it in a garden-pot, "and o'er it set sweet basil, which her tears kept ever wet."

Her brothers, wondering why she "sat drooping by the basil green," and "weeping through her hair," contrived to steal the pot and examine it, and then the secret which had been so well kept, was revealed, and Lorenzo's face, "vile with green and livid spot," was before them, and they fled away from Florence, while Isabel, deprived of her treasured basil, "pined and died forlorn, imploring for her basil to the last."

This was the story which touched the artist in his early days, and which he resolved to illustrate; but years passed away ere he was able to carry out his intention, and it was not until 1867 that the picture was completed.

It is a marvel of fine painting, extraordinary science, and conscientious labour. Its colouring is a triumph of skill, startling in its force and the proof it affords of boundless command of means. In colour-scheme, it evidently in some subtle manner is supposed to correspond with the strange, lurid ideas of the story, or to produce the effect that is given by the line—

"vile with green and livid spot";

and in this way it is very remarkable.

The "power, learning, colour, skill, and certainty of effect," as a great critic has said of this picture, mark it as an important work; but when this is said, candour demands that praise be taken no further.

It is impossible to think that the Isabel who appears in the picture with her healthy and vigorous appearance is the heroine of Keats' poem, or that she can be the melancholy, dreamy, pitying, weeping, damsel of whom the poem speaks.

The grouping may be dexterous, and the scheme of colour marvellous, but the poetry of the original conception in the poem is not to be found in the painting, and the emotion created in the poem with the deep pity which the reader can hardly fail to have for " poor, simple Isabel," will never be produced by the sight of this picture.

The work is a good example of the want of poetic imagination on the part of the artist—the want of true sympathy with such a delicate and touching episode in life.

There is not a trace of the frenzy of ideal attachment in the picture, of the tenderness and depth of a love which refuses in so poetic a manner to accept death, and there is a lack of idealism and a want of the knowledge of the more subtle anatomy of human expression clearly apparent in it.

It is as important in considering a painter that we should understand the reasons for his failures as the causes which make for his success ; it is always desirable that we should bear in mind that his capacity is strictly limited, and that the artist himself is not often the one who best can diagnose his own capabilities, and so occasionally attempts a theme which is beyond his powers to treat.

It will, we think, be allowed that we have an instance of this in the picture before us, and it gives us a striking lesson in considering the work of the artist.

The remaining two works are upon the older

THE SHADOW OF DEATH.

lines—Scriptural in their origin, didactic in their aim, and symbolic in their teaching.

The Shadow of Death, which was begun in 1868, is a large and noble work. It adorns the end of a great gallery in the Permanent Exhibition in Manchester, having been presented to that city by Messrs. Agnew, and cannot fail to rouse attention from even the most indifferent of spectators.

To use the artist's own words, "the picture represents our Lord as the Man Christ gaining His bread by the sweat of His brow ; presenting Him to our view subjected to the ordinary conditions of man's nature, and compelled to realize in His own person the effect of the curse pronounced upon Adam and his posterity.

"The Virgin Mother is represented as looking over the gifts of the Magi—gifts doubtless treasured up with all a mother's care ; and who can tell the amount of the knowledge vouchsafed to her of the frightful doom of the working Lord ? Her attitude tells of her fright and terror, though her features are not portrayed. The shadow of the wearied Lord falling on the rack which holds the carpenter's tools, with the mandrel placed vertically in the centre, at once literally realizes the form of a cross, and the hands falling thereon suggest the idea of a figure nailed thereupon, and thus the particular death our Lord would die— the 'shadow of the death !'"

In considering this great work it must be borne in mind that the idea of the artist was to depict our Lord as He would have appeared when, as a

man, He worked in His home in the Holy Land
at the bench in His cottage.　Hence the figure is
that of a well-built Eastern carpenter, and all the
details of the picture, painted as they were in the
East, are accurate representations of what would
be found in a workshop in those days, and which
in the "unchanging East" are to be seen still.

The picture must be judged from another
standard than that of a mere painting.　Every
detail has been the subject of profound study
—the tools and the gifts, the ivory chest, the
costume in all its varying items, the dwelling, the
view from the windows, the foliage, the trestles,
the timber, and the bench, to say nothing of the
wonderful face and the magnificent figure—all are
painted with perfect accuracy, honest purpose, and
the most punctilious attention to truth.

That this is so, must always be carefully remembered when the picture is seen, and most of all
when it is criticised, as in the light of its truth
many of the strange effects of colour, which jar
upon the sensitive spectator may be condoned.

We are so much in the habit of considering the
events of sacred story as though they had taken
place either in our own country, or else under the
Italian treatment given to pictures of them by
the chief of the Old Masters, that we forget the
actual surroundings which environed our Lord in
His life upon earth, and do not sufficiently realize
the difference which exists between Oriental and
Occidental life in every way.

The heightened colour which is to be found
upon the ruddy skin of the stalwart figure before us,

the long black, matted hair, the gay-coloured loin-cloth, are characteristic of the Oriental workman, and although unfamiliar to our eyes, are none the less true on that account.

We grant a certain element of melodrama—it is inseparable from the art of Holman Hunt; but that accepted, there are many fine features in this great work which will repay examination.

The chief fault—and it is one which constantly occurs, and which must not be overlooked—is, that while it is needful to insist upon the exact representation of details in art, yet it is equally important that each detail should be considered in relative proportion to its importance with regard to the given subject.

It is harmony which is desired, and it is the want of this which so often troubles us in the pictures painted by Mr. Holman Hunt. In the present case the insistence upon the exact repre-sentation of the shavings upon the floor has injured the total effect of the picture, and the too hard and definite painting, with rigid accuracy, of the fittings of the workshop serves, in a measure, to detract from the full dignity of the central figure.

At the same time, in technique it is extra-ordinarily fine. The whole thing is built up solidly, steadily, and without flinching, and the result is a fine piece of work, severe, just, impressive, only lacking that pleasing quality of harmony and delight without which no picture can be con-sidered a masterpiece.

The last great work which this artist has submitted to the public is *The Triumph of the Innocents.*

This was first shown in the gallery of the Fine Art Society in Bond Street in the spring of 1885. It had taken more than seven years to conceive and execute, and on that ground alone it would demand consideration and attention.

It is a very fine piece of colour—brilliant, clear, definite. The insistence upon details is not quite so hard as in earlier works, and in that respect the picture gains over those which have been mentioned already. It is as true in its honest accuracy as were any of the other pictures, and it is created in the same pure light with as little atmospheric modulation. In drawing it is one of the best things the artist ever did, and the figure of St. Joseph is especially fine.

There is an impress of the artist's own character upon every part of the work. He, as usual, put himself into his work, produced it with his utmost strength, with the determination to speak his message in unerring accents, so that the world could not fail to hear it.

As a representation of Eastern scenery with Eastern light, the picture is unrivalled, and the imagery of it is original, remarkable, and impressive. Yet with all these superabundant qualities the painting fails in conveying the pleasure that a great work of this sort should always give to the spectator.

The fault is partly in the colour, the crudity of certain tints, the spottiness of others, partly it consists in the flesh - tones, with their over-

By permission of the Corporation of Liverpool.]

THE TRIUMPH OF THE INNOCENTS.

vigorous ruddiness, and partly the error is in the
crowded condition of the canvas and in the
existence of so many interwoven threads of
thought which overwhelm the composition.

The picture is full of imaginative reasoning;
it is powerful, complete, and sincere; but all these
qualities can be found in works of far less merit than
this painting, and works which yet will appeal more
strongly to the emotions than this one can ever do.

The artist himself explained his meaning in
the picture in these words: "The spirits of the
children of Bethlehem troop along by the side of
the Holy Child; they bear the signs of their
martyrdom. Garlanded as were ancient sacri-
fices, and bearing branches of blossoming trees,
like enrolled saints, they appear" in habit "as
they lived, the forward ones already rejoiced in
the knowledge of their high service. Midway
there is an infant, bewildered to find that his
spiritual body bears no trace of the fatal wound.
Behind, in the air, are babes; this sleeping,
grieving group is the only one in the picture
which, in its sorrowing aspect, connects the idea
of human pain with the fate suffered; for the rest,
in degrees differing, death is already seen to have
no sting, the grave no victory."

The stream, said the artist, was "the spiritual,
eternal stream, provided in exchange for the life
that perisheth, which has been to them so brief."
The stream breaks into magnified globes which
"image the thoughts rife in that age, in the minds
of pious Jews, of the millennium."

St. Joseph, anxious to get his dear ones out

of the risk of danger, is hurrying on. He is alarmed by the signal fires and by the noise of the wakeful sheepdogs, and he has no eyes for the supernatural visitors ; but the Child sees His youthful comrades and tries to attract the attention of His mother to them. Her thoughts are fixed upon Him and upon the future, and she does not realize how the company is attended.

It is perhaps in the face and features of the Virgin that the artist has most conspicuously failed. The face which should redeem the picture is commonplace, and too old to agree with the ordinary conception, but it is also the mixture of the real and unreal in the work which is the cause of its failure. The mysteries are not mysterious. The "airy globes" of the description are substantial in form ; the living fountains are semi-transparent, gelatinous material, and the spirituality which the artist has aimed to produce he has not depicted by his pencil, if, indeed, it ever could be so depicted.

The eye at once realizes that the massive forms of the Innocents, with all their garlands and draperies, must be visible to Mary and to Joseph, as they are visible to the spectator, and that there is confusion of idea in the fact which the artist has striven to show that both Mary and Joseph are supremely unaware of the crowd of heavenly visitors who attend them in their journey.

The artist, with his strenuous desire, has again attempted too much, and the result in that respect is failure ; but, nevertheless, there are characteristics in the work that must not be overlooked.

The group of children is as lovely as ever such a group could be. They are all admirable in their fulness of delight and happiness, and would compare favourably with any groups of children that the greater Italian masters ever painted or modelled.

In technique the picture is sound and dexterous, as good as anything that Holman Hunt ever painted, and we may well consider it as his masterpiece; in these respects, a noble work, only prevented from being all that could be wished, by its strange mingling of mystic with commonplace effects, its extraordinary light, its too hard shadows, the inadequate features of the Virgin, and the overcrowded symbolism of the canvas.

LIST OF THE ARTIST'S CHIEF WORKS.

BIRMINGHAM, THE ART GALLERY.

THE TWO GENTLEMEN OF VERONA — Valentine rescuing Sylvia from Proteus. Painted in 1852.

THE FINDING OF THE SAVIOUR IN THE TEMPLE.

SHEFFIELD, THE ART EXHIBITION.

THE TRIUMPH OF THE INNOCENTS. Lent by Mr. J. T. Middlemore.

LIVERPOOL, WALKER ART GALLERY.

THE TRIUMPH OF THE INNOCENTS — the smaller fellow-picture to the one owned by Mr. J. T. Middlemore.

MANCHESTER, THE PERMANENT GALLERY.

THE SHADOW OF DEATH. Painted in 1868-70.

THE HIRELING SHEPHERD. Painted at Ewell in 1851.

OXFORD, KEBLE COLLEGE.

THE LIGHT OF THE WORLD. Painted in 1855.

OXFORD, THE UNIVERSITY GALLERIES.

THE FESTIVAL OF ST. SWITHIN. Royal Academy, 1867.

LONDON BRIDGE ON THE NIGHT OF THE MARRIAGE OF THE PRINCESS OF WALES. 1863-1866.

A CONVERTED BRITISH FAMILY SHELTERING A CHRISTIAN MISSIONARY FROM THE PERSECUTION OF THE DRUIDS. Royal Academy, 1850.

THE PLAINS OF ESDRAELON, ABOVE NAZARETH. Grosvenor Gallery, 1877.

MIRIAM WILKINSON.

THE SLEEPING CITY—PERA. Old Water-Colour Society, 1888.

THE AFTERGLOW IN EGYPT. The smaller fellow-picture, the larger one has a sheaf of corn instead of the cage of pigeons. Grosvenor Gallery, 1877.

Portraits of MR. and MRS. COMBE in pastel. Grosvenor Gallery, 1889.

OXFORD, JESUS COLLEGE.

Portrait of the late CANON JENKINS, called NEW COLLEGE CLOISTER. Royal Academy, 1853.

The rest of the works of the artist are in the hands of private owners, or have remained in his own studio.

Mr. Holman Hunt has retained many works, including :

MAY DAY ON MAGDALEN TOWER. Small original finished study and large completed picture.

THE SHIP.

AMARYLLIS.

SACRED FIRE IN THE CHURCH OF THE HOLY SEPULCHRE, JERUSALEM.

BERNE.

ATHENS.

SUNSET IN THE VAL D' ARNO.

THE LADY OF SHALOTT.

A FESTA AT FIESOLE.

THE BIRTHDAY.

The portraits of PROFESSOR OWEN, CYRIL B. HOLMAN HUNT, HILARY HOLMAN HUNT the tracer, DANTE GABRIEL ROSSETTI, A LADY, and others.

Sir Cuthbert Quilter owns *The Scapegoat;* Sir A. H. Fairbairn *The Awakening Conscience;* Mr. George L. Craik *The Wandering Sheep*—which has also been called in exhibitions *Fairlight Downs, Our English Coasts* (under which title it was sent to the Royal Academy in 1853), and *The Strayed Sheep : Sorrow* (one of the finest works of the artist)—*Interior of Salerno Cathedral*, and a drawing on wood called *Rebekah ;* Mr. T. Brocklebank owns *Il Dolce far niente ;* Mrs. Ashton *Claudio and Isabella ;* Mr. James Hall *Isabella and the Pot of Basil ;* Mrs. Holt the smaller version of *The Finding of Christ in the Temple ;* Mr. Middlemore *Christ among the Doctors* and *The Apple Harvest ;* Right Hon. J. Kenrick *The Lanternmaker's Courtship ;* Mr. Haslam the splendid *Bride of Bethlehem ;* Mr. Morse his own portrait, *Asparagus Island,* and a *View from the Mount of Olives ;* Mr. Abraham Haworth and Mr. Jesse Haworth four very fine Eastern landscapes ; Mr. Clarke the interesting early work called *Rienzi vowing to obtain Justice for the Death of his Young Brother,* which was exhibited at the Royal Academy in 1849 ; and Mr. W. M. Rossetti a still earlier picture called *Little Nell and her Grandfather,* painted in 1846, also several other small works and studies by the artist.

Other persons own landscapes and portraits by the artist and smaller water-colour paintings.

MISSING PICTURES

There are a certain number of early works which have been lost sight of by the artist and his friends, and the writer of this book would be glad to hear of any of them. They are especially :

"HARK !" Exhibited in the Royal Academy, 1846, the first work which the artist sent in.

SCENE FROM WOODSTOCK. Dr. Rochecliffe performing Divine Service in the cottage of Joceline Joliffe at Woodstock. Exhibited at the Royal Academy, 1847 ; the second work sent in. 26 × 24.

THE EVE OF ST. AGNES, or THE FLIGHT OF MADELINE AND PORPHYRO. Royal Academy, 1848. 45 × 31. Sold in 1859, and again in 1861. The third work exhibited at the Royal Academy.

JERUSALEM BY MOONLIGHT. Royal Academy, 1856. Graham sale, 1894. 8 × 14.

THE SPHINX. Royal Academy, 1856. Windus sale, 1862.

THE KING OF HEARTS. A boy as Henry VIII. Royal Academy, 1863. Sold in 1872.

MOONLIGHT AT SALERNO. Old Water-Colour Society, 1869.

INTERIOR OF THE MOSQUE OF OMAR. Old Water-Colour Society, 1871.

THE PATHLESS WATER. Old Water-Colour Society, 1871.

WINTER ; AFTERNOON ; SUSSEX DOWNS ; PENZANCE. All exhibited at the Old Water-Colour Society, 1883-84.

THE ARCHIPELAGO. Old Water-Colour Society, 1884-85.

Will-o'-the-wisp; Ivybridge; The Foal of an Ass; Road over the Downs. All exhibited at the Old Water-Colour Society, 1886.

The Haunt of the Gazelle. Old Water-Colour Society, 1889.

"Oh, Pearl," quoth I, etc. Old Water-Colour Society, 1890.

Miss Flamborough. Grosvenor Gallery, 1882.

The School-girl's Hymn. The French Gallery, 1859.

Portraits of Mr. Martineau and Mr. J. B. Price.

Any of the eleven pictures exhibited at the Old Water-Colour Society, 1892-93.

The larger version of The Afterglow in Egypt. 74 × 34. Sold in 1891.

The smaller sketch of The Scapegoat, once belonging to Lord Brassey.

Sunset on the Sea. Sold in 1897.

Morning Prayer. Sold in 1898.

Bianca. 26 × 24. Sold in 1871.

Past and Present. 24 × 18. Sold in 1874.

Dead Mallard. Exhibited at Suffolk Street, 1847.

BOOKS AND ARTICLES ON HOLMAN HUNT

THERE has never been any book issued on the artist which has dealt with his entire career, as he has hitherto refused permission for the necessary information to be given. He is understood to have been engaged for the past thirty years upon an exhaustive work upon the Pre-Raphaelite Brotherhood, which is to contain, when issued, a full and exhaustive life of himself.

The only book which can be recommended as thoroughly reliable deals with the early part of the life of the artist, and is called "W. Holman Hunt and his Works," by F. G. Stephens ; Nisbet, 1860.

The chief account of the work of Holman Hunt is to be found in a series of articles which he contributed to the *Contemporary Review*, 1886, called "The P.R.B. : a Fight for Art," and in similar articles on his pictures in the same review, notably :

"May Day, Magdalen Tower," by Farrar.
"Christ amongst the Doctors," by the artist.
"Religion and Art," by the artist.
"Painting the Scapegoat," by the artist.
"Reminiscences of John Leech," by the artist.
An *Art Annual* for 1893 was issued from the

Art Journal office, which is important as containing a great deal of interesting matter and several fine illustrations; and there are notable articles respecting him to be found in the pages of the *Times, Athenæum, Spectator, Portfolio, Fine Art Quarterly, Magazine of Art, Tinsley's, Macmillan's, Fraser's, Good Words, Fortnightly,* and also articles by himself in the *Magazine of Art* and *New Review.*

Reference should be made to the works of Ruskin; to a pamphlet by A. Gordon Crawford, on the exhibition of Holman Hunt's works, in 1886, at the Gallery of the Fine Art Society; to the catalogue of the same exhibition; and to the various works on Millais, Rossetti, Ruskin, and Tennyson, in which he is mentioned.

His black-and-white work is mentioned in Gleeson White's book on "English Illustration in the Sixties" and in Layard's "Tennyson and his Pre-Raphaelite Illustrators."

He has himself written a work called "The Obligations of the Universities towards Art"; Oxford, 1895.

"English Contemporary Art," by Sizeranne, and Muther's "Modern Painting," contain admirable critical notices of the artist and his work.

BILLING AND SONS, LTD., PRINTERS, GUILDFORD.

The British Artists Series.

*Large post 8vo, in special bindings, with 90 to 100
Illustrations, 7s. 6d. net each.*

Sir Edward Burne-Jones, Bart.

By MALCOLM BELL.

Seventh Edition.

Sir J. E. Millais, Bart., P.R.A.

By A. LYS BALDRY.

Second Edition.

Frederic, Lord Leighton, P.R.A.

By ERNEST RHYS.

Fourth Edition.

The
English Pre-Raphaelite Painters.

Their Associates and Successors.

By PERCY BATE.

Second Edition.

LONDON: GEORGE BELL & SONS.

I

Great Masters in Painting and Sculpture.

Edited by G. C. WILLIAMSON, Litt.D.

Post 8vo, each with 40 illustrations and photogravure frontispiece. 5s. net.

BERNARDINO LUINI. By G. C. Williamson, Litt.D.
VELASQUEZ. By R. A. M. Stevenson.
ANDREA DEL SARTO. By H. Guinness.
LUCA SIGNORELLI. By Maud Cruttwell.
RAPHAEL. By H. Strachey.
CARLO CRIVELLI. By G. McNeil Rushforth, **M.A.**
CORREGGIO. By Selwyn Brinton, M.A.
DONATELLO. By Hope Rea.
PERUGINO. By G. C. Williamson, Litt.D.
SODOMA. By the Contessa Lorenzo Priuli-Bon.
DELLA ROBBIA. By the Marchesa Burlamacchi.
GIORGIONE. By Herbert Cook, M.A.
MEMLINC. By W. H. James Weale.
PIERO DELLA FRANCESCA. By W. G. Waters, **M.A.**
PINTORICCHIO. By Evelyn March Phillipps.
FRANCIA. By George C. Williamson, Litt.D.
BRUNELLESCHI. By Leader Scott.
MANTEGNA. By Maud Cruttwell.
REMBRANDT. By Malcolm Bell.
GIOTTO. By F. Mason Perkins.

In preparation:

WILKIE. By Lord Ronald Sutherland Gower, **M.A., F.S.A.**
DURER. By Hans W. Singer, M.A., Ph.D.
GERARD DOU. By Dr. W. Martin.
TINTORETTO. By J. B. Stoughton Holborn, M.A.
EL GRECO. By Manuel B. Cossio, Litt.D., Ph.D.
PAOLO VERONESE. By Roger E. Fry.
GAUDENZIO FERRARI. By Ethel Halsey.
LEONARDO DA VINCI. By Edward McCurdy, M.A.
WATTEAU & HIS SCHOOL. By Edgecumbe Staley, **B.A.**

Others to follow.

Messrs. Bell's Books.

Bell's Handbooks of the Great Craftsmen.

Illustrated Monographs, biographical and critical, of the Great Craftsmen and Workers of Ancient and Modern Times.

EDITED BY G. C. WILLIAMSON, LITT.D.

Imperial 16mo, profusely illustrated, 5s. net each.

The Pavement Masters of Siena.

By R. H. HOBART CUST, M.A.

Peter Vischer, Bronze Founder.

By CECIL HEADLAM.

The Ivory Workers of the Middle Ages.

By A. M. CUST.

OTHER VOLUMES TO FOLLOW.

3

Messrs. Bell's Books.

Bell's Cathedral Series.

Profusely Illustrated.

*In specially designed cloth cover, crown 8vo,
1s. 6d. net each.*

Now Ready.

BRISTOL.	NORWICH.
CANTERBURY.	OXFORD.
CARLISLE.	PETERBOROUGH.
CHESTER.	RIPON.
CHICHESTER.	ROCHESTER.
DURHAM.	ST. DAVID'S.
ELY.	ST. PAUL'S.
EXETER.	SALISBURY.
GLOUCESTER.	SOUTHWELL.
HEREFORD.	WELLS.
LICHFIELD.	WINCHESTER.
LINCOLN.	YORK.
MANCHESTER.	WORCESTER.

In Preparation.

ST. ALBANS.	ST. ASAPH **AND**
LLANDAFF.	BANGOR.
GLASGOW.	

Bell's Cathedral Series—*continued.*

The following uniform Volumes are also published,
1s. 6d. net each.

ST. MARTIN'S CHURCH, CANTERBURY.

BEVERLEY MINSTER.

TEWKESBURY ABBEY AND DEERHURST
 PRIORY.

CHRISTCHURCH PRIORY AND WIMBORNE
 ABBEY.

BATH ABBEY, MALMESBURY ABBEY, AND
 BRADFORD-ON-AVON CHURCH.

WESTMINSTER ABBEY.

ENGLISH CATHEDRALS. An Itinerary and
 Description.

Bell's Handbooks to Continental Churches.

Profusely Illustrated. Crown 8vo, 2s. 6d. net each.

CHARTRES : THE CATHEDRAL, and other
 Churches.

ROUEN : THE CATHEDRAL, and other Churches.

AMIENS.

PARIS : NOTRE DAME. [*Preparing.*

Life and Light Books.

Prettily Bound, 1s. net each.

1. THE GREATEST THING EVER KNOWN. By RALPH WALDO TRINE, author of "In Tune with the Infinite." *16th Thousand.*

2. FATE MASTERED—DESTINY FULFILLED. By W. J. COLVILLE, author of "The World's Fair Text-book of Mental Therapeutics."

3. EVERY LIVING CREATURE, or Heart-Training through the Animal World. By RALPH WALDO TRINE.

4. LEGENDS AND LYRICS. By ADELAIDE A. PROCTER. *130th Thousand.* First Series.

5. LEGENDS AND LYRICS. By ADELAIDE A. PROCTER. Second Series.

6. BILLY AND HANS: My Squirrel Friends. A True History. By W. J. STILLMAN.

7. KITH AND KIN: Poems of Animal Life selected by HENRY S. SALT.

8. CHARACTER-BUILDING: Thought Power. By RALPH WALDO TRINE.

9. LIGHT FROM THE EAST. Selections from the Teaching of the Buddha. By EDITH WARD.

10. PARABLES FROM NATURE. A Selection. By MRS. M. GATTY.

11. BETTER FOOD FOR BOYS. By EUSTACE H. MILES, author of "Muscle, Brain, and Diet."

12. MATHEMATICAL LAW IN THE SPIRITUAL WORLD. By EUSTACE H. MILES.

OTHERS TO FOLLOW.

Messrs. Bell's Books.

The Chiswick Shakespeare.

Illustrated by BYAM SHAW.

With Introductions and Glossaries by
JOHN DENNIS.

Pott 8vo, cloth, 1s. 6d. net each; or limp leather, 2s. net.

HAMLET.
AS YOU LIKE IT.
OTHELLO.
MACBETH.
THE MERCHANT OF VENICE.
THE TEMPEST.
ROMEO AND JULIET.
THE WINTER'S TALE.
KING JOHN.
KING LEAR.
MIDSUMMER NIGHT'S DREAM.
TWELFTH NIGHT.
RICHARD II.
CORIOLANUS.
MUCH ADO ABOUT NOTHING.

ANTONY AND CLEOPATRA.
TWO GENTLEMEN OF VERONA.
JULIUS CÆSAR.
KING HENRY IV. Part I.
KING HENRY IV. Part II.
KING HENRY V.
CYMBELINE.
THE MERRY WIVES OF WINDSOR.
LOVE'S LABOUR'S LOST.
MEASURE FOR MEASURE.
KING HENRY VI. Part I.
KING HENRY VI. Part II.
KING HENRY VI. Part III.

Further Volumes at Monthly intervals.

LONDON: GEORGE BELL & SONS.
YORK STREET, COVENT GARDEN.
8